REVIEW COPY

Mario Lemieux

Mario Lemieux

Star Center

Ken Rappoport

Enslow Publishers, Inc.

44 Fadem Road	PO Box 38
Box 699	Aldershot
Springfield, NJ 07081	Hants GU12 6BP
USA	UK

For my mother, forever young.

Library of Congress Cataloging-in-Publication Data

Rappoport, Ken.
    Mario Lemieux : star center / Ken Rappoport.
        p. cm. — (Sports reports)
    Includes index.
    Summary: Details the life and career of the top-scoring hockey superstar
who led the Pittsburgh Penguins to two Stanley Cup championships.
    ISBN 0-89490-932-0
    1. Lemieux, Mario, 1965- —Juvenile literature. 2. Hockey players—
Canada—Biography—Juvenile literature. 3. Pittsburgh Penguins (Hockey
team)—Juvenile literature. [1. Lemieux, Mario, 1965- . 2. Hockey players.]
I. Title. II. Series.
GV848.5.L46R35   1998
796.962'092—dc21
[B]   97-49431
                                             CIP
                                             AC

Printed in the United States of America

10 9 8 7 6 5 4 3 2 1

Photo Credits: Andre Viau, Journal de Montreal, p. 30; AP/Wide World
Photos, pp. 10, 13, 44, 47, 55, 64, 66, 70, 76, 83, 87, 88, 93, 98; John Taylor,
Journal de Montreal, pp. 21, 25, 35; Luc Belisle, Journal de Montreal, p. 36;
P.Y. Pelletier, Journal de Montreal, p. 23; Willie Lapointe, Journal de
Montreal, p. 32.

Cover Photo: AP/Wide World Photos

Contents

Chapter 1

Back From the Brink

Mario Lemieux tightened his seat belt and looked out the window as his chartered plane circled the Philadelphia International Airport. From the first time he touched a puck in the National Hockey League (NHL) in 1984, the Pittsburgh Penguins' center was a special player. He was known as Super Mario. At six foot four and 226 pounds, Lemieux's grace and puck-handling skills were unequaled for a player his size. Few players were more feared by goaltenders.

But now it was Lemieux who felt fear. Lemieux was a six-time NHL scoring champion and three-time most valuable player with two Stanley Cups to his credit. Now, though, he was scared. He had been diagnosed with cancer. He missed hockey desperately while he was fighting for his life. This would be the first time in nearly two months he would be playing in an NHL game.

Lemieux had completed his twenty-second and final radiation treatment in a Pittsburgh hospital on the morning of March 2, 1993. The treatments had sapped his strength and left him in a weakened condition, but he was upbeat. He had waited so long for this moment. Tonight he was coming back to the game he loved.

But Lemieux was at a severe disadvantage. Just a few days' layoff can throw a player off his stride. Lemieux had missed a total of twenty-three games. Now he would be playing against a tough arch-rival, the Philadelphia Flyers, at the Spectrum in Philadelphia.

In the locker room, Lemieux was quiet as he dressed—more quiet than usual. He slipped on a black turtleneck to protect the sensitive area around his neck. He had been warmly greeted by his teammates. They could not help but notice the reddened area that looked like a bad sunburn. This was the result of radiation treatments after the tumor had been removed from his neck.

Then it was game time. It was time to go out and face the Flyers and their raucous fans, who usually booed the opposition. But when the towering

Lemieux skated onto the ice in his black and gold Penguins uniform, something unusual happened. Cheers erupted throughout the building. "Mar-i-o! Mar-i-o!" As the electronic scoreboard flashed "Welcome Back," the fans were standing, actually applauding an opposing player. The unexpected support lifted his spirits.

Lemieux skated out to center ice to join his teammates for the pregame national anthem. The growing cheers of the crowd showed no signs of stopping. Lemieux acknowledged the thunderous welcome by raising his white stick high in the air. It was good to be back.

Lemieux was back at his familiar center position. He did not know what to expect, but he was glad to be off the sidelines. His first shift lasted less than a minute, but he was back in the flow of it. Now could he get back onto the scoring sheet?

From personal experience, the Flyers knew only too well the kind of damage Lemieux could cause on the ice. In the 1989 playoffs the Penguins and Flyers were locked in a fierce struggle, tied 2–2 after the first four games of their seven-game series. Lemieux had been in a slump and hurting, suffering from head, neck, and knee injuries sustained in a loss to Philadelphia in Game 4.

Never more determined, Lemieux took the ice

Mario Lemieux (foreground) was quick to get back into the flow of the game upon returning to the ice after a long absence.

for Game 5 and simply played one of the greatest games in Penguins history. Quickly, he scored on a breakaway. Then another. A third goal came off a pass from defenseman Paul Coffey. He scored three goals in less than seven minutes.

Before the first period was over, the big, sharp-shooting center with the long, loping strides had added a fourth. He was on his way to a record-tying eight-point game. (A player receives a point for every goal and for every assist that helps to set up a teammate's goal.) He finished off his night with a fifth goal into an empty net as the Penguins beat the Flyers 10–7.

Lemieux had always been a powerful force on the ice. With his deft stick-handling and seeming ability to score almost at will, he was unstoppable. But throughout the first period of his return game on March 2, 1993, he failed to register either a goal or an assist as the Penguins fell behind. The rugged Flyers were keeping him caged in, and he was desperately trying to break out.

By the second period, the Penguins were losing, 3–1. The Flyers were playing their typical hard-hitting game. The weakened Lemieux was hardly up to his usual standard of play. But when he found the puck on his stick deep in the left faceoff circle, he suddenly found new strength. With lightning speed, he ripped a sharply angled shot toward the net. The puck flew past the stunned goaltender and the red light above the net flashed. Score! It was a brilliant play. Despite suffering from fatigue and clearly playing at less than full strength, Lemieux had scored his fortieth goal of the season.

Less than two minutes later, Lemieux again controlled the puck. This time, instead of shooting it, he spotted Kevin Stevens open. With a quick flick of his wrist, he fired a pass to his teammate. Stevens scored to tie the game at 3 goals.

Despite Lemieux's performance, the Penguins lost, 5–4. Still, the night belonged to Mario the Magnificent. It was a miraculous performance. Lemieux demonstrated his courage by just being on the ice. He was determined that nothing—not the fog that had canceled his commercial flight, not his medical problems, nor his radiation treatments—would stop him. "How can you imagine what he did?" Kevin Stevens asked. "It's unbelievable . . . crazy. Only one person in the world could have done what he did."[1]

Overcoming the odds was nothing new for Mario Lemieux. The Penguins had also needed a miracle in 1984 when Lemieux joined them as an eighteen-year-old rookie. For two years, they had been the worst team with the worst attendance in

The Pittsburgh Penguins' players and fans were overjoyed to have Mario Lemieux back in action and contributing to the team's success once again.

the NHL. There were rumors they might move out of town. Enter Mario Lemieux. He had been the most talked about player in the team's history. But could a French Canadian star who was only eighteen years old save a franchise? It did not seem possible. The obstacles seemed overwhelming.

Lemieux was a stranger. He had come to the United States from a French-speaking part of Canada. He had difficulty speaking and understanding English. He was facing a new culture, trying to adjust to life in America. His veteran teammates were skeptical. What was this new kid with

FACT

NHL records held by Mario Lemieux:

- Most short-handed goals in a season (13 in 1988–89)
- Most career overtime goals (9)
- Most overtime points in a career (19)
- Highest goals-per-game average in a career (.825)
- Most points in an All-Star Game (6 in 1988)
- Most goals in a period (4 against Montreal on Jan. 26, 1997, tied with 10 others)

the big-money contract going to show them? Every team, every opponent on the ice, would be out to get him. This was not going to be easy.

So what did Lemieux do? The rookie scored 100 points on 43 goals and 57 assists. Then he won the Calder Memorial Trophy as the NHL's top rookie. Suddenly, the Penguins were selling out games. Fans loved him. His dazzling play sparked a fan explosion in Pittsburgh.

Lemieux went on to steal the spotlight at the NHL All-Star Game that season, playing against such greats as Wayne Gretzky and Marcel Dionne. The teenage Lemieux was named the Most Valuable Player (MVP) over NHL veteran players he had admired all his life.

This was not the first time Lemieux had dominated a hockey rink. He had been the center of attention since he was a young boy.

Chapter 2

A Mighty Mite

With the wind whistling in their faces like a slap shot, Mario Lemieux and his friends headed for the snow-covered pond at the old church. As they passed through the working-class neighborhood of Ville Emard on the outskirts of Montreal, Canada, they had their skates slung over their shoulders and shovels tucked under their arms.

Skating was a passion for Mario Lemieux. It had been, ever since he was a three-year-old coached by his father. Day after day, Jean-Guy Lemieux would bring his son to a nearby rink and teach him the fundamentals of hockey.

Now, as a grade-school student, Mario rarely missed a day of practice—no matter how severe the weather. When the youngsters reached the pond, they started to shovel the snow off to the sides. It took them an hour before they could skate. Then Mario and his friends formed two teams and played for hours as the sun melted low into the Canadian horizon.

When the snow was too deep and the winds too severe, the Lemieuxs found another way for Mario to play. Jean-Guy filled his front hallway with snow and packed it down so that Mario and his two brothers, Alain and Richard, could skate indoors.

In French, *le mieux* means "the best." This was an appropriate description of Mario Lemieux, who appeared to have been born with a hockey stick in his hands. Mario Lemieux was born on October 5, 1965, in Montreal, Quebec, Canada. His father, Jean-Guy, was a construction worker until a back problem forced him into early retirement. He was tall and quiet, the opposite of his petite, outspoken wife, Pierrette. Mario was more like his dad.

Mario Lemieux exhibited unusual hockey skills from a very young age. He was so talented that his father decided to enroll him in a league for eight- to ten-year-olds. The problem was, Mario was not even six years old yet.

Jean-Guy brought his son down to the rink to introduce him to the coach of the Ville Emard Hurricanes, the popular local Mighty Mite team.

How old is he?" the coach asked Lemieux's father. "Almost six," his father responded "Too young. He's got to be eight," said the coach. "He's big for his age. Give him a chance," Mario's father pleaded.[1]

The coach sent Mario out to take the game's opening faceoff. Five-year-old Mario, playing against players almost twice his age, took control of the puck. Confidently, the youngster skated the length of the ice and scored. His father did not have to say another word. Mario made the team.

As Mario grew, he began filling the net with pucks and leading his teams to championships. Trophy after trophy filled his bedroom. Stories about his exploits filled scrapbooks. A photograph displayed proudly in his bedroom showed twelve-year-old Lemieux being presented a trophy by one of his heroes, Montreal Canadiens superstar Guy Lafleur. Mario was only twelve when National Hockey League scouts from the Philadelphia Flyers and Vancouver Canucks came to Quebec to see him play.

At thirteen, playing in a bantam league featuring thirteen- to fifteen-year-old players, Mario scored an amazing 130 goals in just 32 games. "I can remember always being able to score, even from the time I was in pee wee [nine- and ten-year-olds]," Lemieux said. "It had to be a natural talent because it seemed like every time I shot the puck it went in. I always finished first in scoring."[2]

Mario was an intense competitor. He hated to lose, whether it was at hockey or the board game of Monopoly™. In the summer, Mario and his friends would play basement hockey with a tennis ball. "If Mario lost, it would be as if a hurricane went through the basement," his father said.[3]

To live in Montreal was to be a Canadiens fan and Mario was certainly no exception. He followed every win and loss for the Canadiens, as did most of the youngsters—and adults—who resided in Quebec Province. Mario's father, who had played amateur hockey, took him to many of the Canadiens' games. At the Montreal Forum, a wide-eyed Mario watched his heroes perform. And perform they did, winning championship after championship.

When he could not go to games, there was always television. One Saturday night he and his brothers wanted to watch *Hockey Night in Canada*, the weekly national broadcast of a featured game from the National Hockey League. The baby-sitter insisted on watching a movie. It was a decision she soon regretted. She found herself locked in the bathroom, as Mario and his brothers settled in for the night and watched their hockey game.[4]

FACT

Some of the things Mario Lemieux likes other than hockey:

- Golf
- Video games
- Doing impressions of Elvis Presley and comic Pee-wee Herman

Lemieux was determined to follow the path of his older brother, Alain, who had set his sights on playing in the NHL. Lemieux's other brother, Richard, had dropped out of hockey at the age of fourteen because it stopped being fun for him.

Mario was having more fun than ever. He scored 62 goals as a fifteen-year-old in the midget ranks. He was ready for the next step—the Canadian juniors. The juniors are the highest amateur hockey level in Canada. They are a breeding ground for the NHL much like the minor leagues are for major-league baseball. There are three major junior leagues in Canada: the Western Hockey League (WHL), the Ontario Hockey League (OHL), and the Quebec Major Junior Hockey League (QMJHL). Lemieux was the first pick of the Laval Voisins of the QMJHL.

Lemieux set some goals: winning a team championship for Laval and a scoring championship for himself. He had his work cut out. The Voisins had finished last the year before. In Lemieux's first season, the Voisins immediately jumped a couple of spots in the standings and began filling their arena to capacity. In his second season, the Voisins were on top of the league.

Lemieux's dream of a scoring championship had to wait. There were sixteen players who scored more points than Lemieux in his first year at Laval. In his

Lemieux wore the uniform of the Laval Voisins with pride. Naturally, a hockey stick was never far from his side.

second year, when he was sixteen years old, he made a decision. His goal was to be the No. 1 pick in the NHL draft. But he was having difficulty handling school and hockey. There were long bus trips on his hockey schedule. The trips from Laval to Chicoutimi were especially difficult. Mario never looked forward to the five-hour bus ride to play the Saugeneens. "We'd leave very early in the morning," Lemieux said, "travel five hours on a bus, play the game and then leave for home right after the game. And then have to wake up for school the next morning."[5]

His solution was to quit school and devote his full time and energy to hockey. He was sure that he would make it as a professional hockey player. "I wanted to be able to skate in the morning and play hockey at night without being tired for the game, and I figured I could do my learning through living and traveling," he said.[6]

Lemieux's father was against it. Jean-Guy Lemieux wanted his son to finish school. When Mario held firm to his decision, his father eventually relented.

"Finally he agreed with me that I should concentrate on hockey because I was only two years away from the draft," Lemieux said.[7]

Lemieux's performance in his second year of

Having difficulty balancing his hockey schedule with his education, Mario dropped out of school to concentrate full-time on his duties with Laval.

juniors picked up. He was proud of his excellent 1982–83 season at Laval. He had 84 goals and 100 assists for 184 points. Still, he was overshadowed by Pat LaFontaine, a spunky, five-foot ten-inch American center who scored 234 points for Verdun.

Finishing runner-up was difficult for Lemieux to accept. He had been scoring champion everywhere he played. Now he had missed out for two straight years. He had almost tripled his goal total in his second season at Laval from 30 to 84. Still, he was not in sight of the runaway LaFontaine, who was stealing all of the headlines.

FACT

Pittsburgh Penguins records held by Mario Lemieux:

- Most goals (85), assists (114), and points (199) in a season
- Most goals (5-three times), assists (6-three times), and points (8-twice) in a game
- Most hat tricks in a season (9) and career (39)
- Most career goals (613), assists (881), points (1,494), power-play goals (201), game-winning goals (65), short-handed goals (47), and shots on goal (3,054)
- Longest goal streak (12 games, Oct. 6–Nov. 1, 1992)
- Longest assist streak (14 games, Jan. 15–Feb. 16, 1986)
- Longest point streak (46 games, Oct. 31, 1989–Feb. 11, 1990)

Mario Lemieux sends the puck past the goaltender, putting another point on the board for Laval.

Adding to Lemieux's frustration was a bitter experience in Leningrad, Russia, at the world junior championships. His first international experience was one of the worst of his hockey career. There was reported friction with coach Dave King, who had assigned him a minor role on the team. Injuries reduced his playing time even more. He also missed four games at Laval, where he had hopes of catching LaFontaine in the scoring race. He wondered if it was worth all the trouble to represent his country on the world stage.

Lemieux's team had won a championship, but he had lost the scoring race. Lemieux had one more season in Canadian juniors, and this time, LaFontaine was not in the picture. The Verdun star had left, and Lemieux would have the stage all to himself. Could he rise to the challenge?

Chapter 3

Chasing the Record

What was motivating Mario Lemieux? He was scoring goals and practicing every day. It had everything to do with the goal-scoring record of his idol, Guy Lafleur. In the 1971–72 season, Lafleur had scored 130 goals for the Quebec Ramparts of the QMJHL. No one had ever come close to that staggering figure in Canada's junior ranks. It was thought that no one ever would—until Lemieux began his assault on the record book in the 1983–84 season. Lemieux was also shooting for Pierre Larouche's season point record of 251.

After just twenty-three games, Lemieux had scored an incredible 99 points on 44 goals and 55 assists. That put him on track for the league's goal- and point-scoring records. Nothing could stop

Lemieux, it seemed. Not even the Canadian government.

In the midst of his charge at the record books, Lemieux found himself in the middle of a controversy that made headlines across Canada. An invitation came to play for Team Canada at the world juniors in Sweden. Bitter memories remained of Lemieux's international experience from the previous year. The Christmas-week tournament would wipe out four games at Laval—four precious games he would need to rewrite the record books. He declined the invitation. His decision triggered widespread disapproval. Lemieux held his ground.

FACT

Mario Lemieux's career stats as a junior player with the Laval Voisons:

Year	Games Played	Goals	Assists	Points	Penalty Minutes
1981–82	64	30	66	96	22
1982–83	66	84	100	184	76
1983–84	70	133	149	282	92

The league decided to punish him. Lemieux was stunned. The league suspended him for four regular-season games and for the QMJHL All-Star Game.

Lemieux went to court. He challenged the suspension as unconstitutional. Lemieux won his case. A Quebec superior court justice ruled that the QMJHL had no legal right to deny Lemieux any playing time at Laval. The Canadian government had no legal right to force him to play in an international tournament. This ruling came despite the fact that the judge personally considered Lemieux's stand morally wrong.[1]

Lemieux was the hottest junior player in the country. He scored at least one point in every game as he continued to extend his record scoring streak. Lemieux was the talk of Canada. He had already broken Larouche's point record of 251, and there were still five games left on the seventy-game schedule. Could he possibly score in every game that season?

However, in Laval's next game against Verdun, an unusual story line was unfolding. The Voisins were leading 3–2 late in the contest and Lemieux had yet to score a point. Credit the ferocious Verdun defense. It was doing everything it could to keep Lemieux off the score sheet. With one minute to go,

While chasing the league scoring record, Mario Lemieux became well known throughout Canada. Here, Lemieux takes time out to greet a young fan.

Verdun coach Pierre Creamer pulled his goaltender for an extra skater. The Verdun fans booed loudly. Normally, they would approve of such a move because it gives their team a manpower advantage. But the fans were afraid that the empty net would give Lemieux a chance to score. Winning the game, it seemed, was not as important to the fans as stopping Lemieux's streak. "It was funny," Creamer said. "As a coach, I was thinking of winning the game. But the crowd wanted us to stop Mario."[2] But no goal was scored and Lemieux had his streak stopped at sixty-five games. Actually, that was the only game of the season in which Lemieux failed to score at least one point.

He had been a model of consistency that season. Like all great players, Lemieux's consistent performance inspired those around him to do better. Jacques Goyette, usually a twenty-goal scorer, became a seventy-goal scorer aided by Lemieux's spectacular passing ability. Chantal Machabee was the Voisins' media representative at the time. She recalls this story about Michel Bourque, a player from eastern Canada who had not scored a goal all season:

> Mario said, "Okay, everybody has to have one goal in a year. Michel, just go in front of the net, put your stick on the ice. Stay there, don't

Each time he stepped on the ice, Mario Lemieux played with an intensity that made Laval a stronger team.

move. I'll control the puck, I'll give it to you and you just have to flip it in the net."

Michel went to the net and didn't move. We were all waiting to see what would happen. When Mario took the puck, he went flying down the ice and passed to Michel. It just tipped on his stick and went into the net. Michel didn't have to move. He didn't do anything. He was just standing there, and he had his first goal of the year. Everyone on the bench was laughing.[3]

Although the Voisins had already clinched the league championship, there was still some serious business left for Lemieux. With four games left, he was still twelve goals behind Lafleur's record of 130. He had been averaging about two a game; now he needed to average three just to tie the record. In the next three games, Lemieux managed nine goals. He needed four in his last game to top Lafleur's mark.

The opponent that night was Longueil. The arena was packed with feverish fans. Chantal Machabee was in the press box with hockey greats Wayne Gretzky and Paul Coffey. They were there to see if Mario could pull off the miracle.

This was pressure. Machabee had talked to Lemieux before the game.

"Are you nervous?"

"No, not that much. I know I'm going to do it."[4]

Forty-three seconds into the game, Lemieux scored his first goal of the night. He was on his way to breaking the record. Less than two minutes later, he scored another. The sellout crowd screamed its approval.

The Longueil defenders could not seem to stop Lemieux. Everything was falling into place. His long reach, his puck-handling skills, and his natural ability to see the entire ice were all coming into play on this night.

The confident Lemieux would not be stopped. He quickly scored another goal off a faceoff, digging the puck away from his opponent and blasting it into the net in almost the same motion. Incredibly, Lemieux had tied Lafleur's record with a hat trick (three goals) in the first period.

Two periods to go. Now all Lemieux needed was one more goal to break the record. A buzz went through the crowd as the second period started. The fans did not have to wait long before Lemieux brought them to their feet.

He roared down the ice on a breakaway with a teammate. Then he deposited the puck into the net with barely seven minutes gone in the period. Lemieux had broken the record—and he had done it with less than half the game completed. Two more goals followed as Lemieux finished with six in all

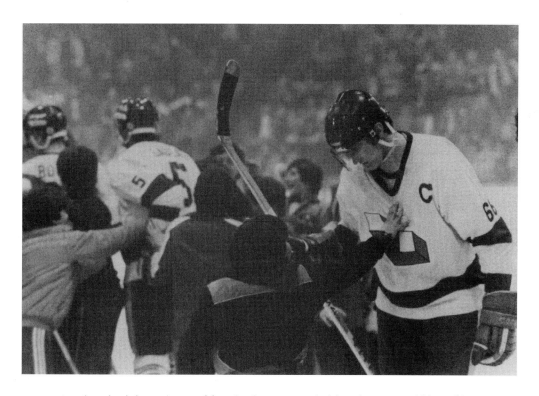

Lemieux had the support of fans both young and old, as he came within striking distance of the league scoring record.

Mario Lemieux, Laval's biggest star, acknowledges the cheers of the appreciative home team fans.

along with five assists, for an incredible 11-point night. His season totals: 133 goals and 149 assists for 282 points.

Then the unexpected followed. Lemieux went flat in the playoffs. The Voisins could not win a game in the Memorial Cup. The tournament decided junior hockey supremacy in Canada.

"He was almost invisible at the Memorial Cup," recalled Herb Zurkowsky of the Montreal Gazette. "He did nothing, which made all of us start to wonder."[5] Doubters were now questioning Lemieux's ability to play in the NHL.

Lemieux was going to be the Pittsburgh Penguins' choice in the NHL draft—No. 1 overall. The Penguins were sure about Lemieux. But the feeling was not necessarily mutual. Even before Lemieux was drafted, the Penguins and Mario Lemieux's agent were talking about his contract. Lemieux was unhappy with what the team was offering. Draft day came on June 9, 1984. The Penguins announced their No. 1 choice. General manager Eddie Johnson stood alone onstage with the Penguins jersey, waiting for Lemieux. He remained alone.

Once again, Lemieux was in the center of controversy. The media called him a "prima donna."

FACT

In the 1984 NHL Entry Draft, Mario Lemieux was selected first overall by the Pittsburgh Penguins. Other players the Penguins selected that year:

Doug Bodger
Roger Belanger
Mark Teevens
Arto Javanainen
Tom Ryan
John Del Col
Steve Hurt
Jim Steen
Mark Ziliotto

Lemieux had battled the courts. Now he was battling an NHL team.

Finally, Lemieux settled on a two-year contract worth $700,000. It was an extravagant contract for a rookie. No first-year player in the NHL had ever been paid that kind of money. Lemieux would have to prove he was worth it.

Chapter 4

The Next Gretzky

Mario Lemieux took the ice for an intrasquad game with his skeptical Pittsburgh Penguins teammates. The Penguins had been losing money, losing games, and losing fans. And along came an eighteen-year-old who walked into camp with a big-money contract—more money than most of them had ever seen—and with a label as the "savior" of the franchise. His teammates were skeptical. Despite all the press clippings, despite all the money, Mario Lemieux had to prove himself.

Lemieux swooped down the ice and received a pass from a teammate. He deftly tapped the puck between the legs of a fast-closing defenseman and quickly whirled around him. Now Lemieux had the puck on his stick in the clear and he was speedily bearing down on goaltender Michel Dion. Before the startled Dion had a chance to react, Lemieux had swept the puck past his glove hand into the net. Four hundred die-hard fans had assembled to watch the new kid perform in the intrasquad game. They broke into wild cheers.

Lemieux was not finished. In the next hour, he showed off a variety of showstopping skills that thrilled the crowd. With his long reach, the rangy Lemieux took the puck off opponents' sticks, dazzled them with his skating and stick-handling abilities and fired perfect passes to teammates. "He did things that only Gretzky can do," said Pittsburgh scout Bruce Haralson. "That's what's scary—to think that there might be another one."[1]

The Pittsburgh Penguin team was badly in need of something positive. Since joining the NHL as an expansion team in 1967, the Penguins' history had been filled, for the most part, with failure, frustration, and tragedy. The Penguins lost one of their top players when Michel Briere, coming off a strong rookie season, died as the result of a car crash in 1970. In 1983, general manager Baz Bastein was also killed in an auto accident.

Nor was fate with them on the ice. The Penguins held a 3–0 lead in a best-of-seven playoff series against the New York Islanders in 1975. They were one game away from advancing to the next round. The Penguins made the record books, but not the way they expected. They suffered through four straight losses. They became only the second team in league history to lose a seven-game playoff series after winning the first three.

Less than two months later, the owners found that their doors had been closed by the authorities. The Penguins became the first team to go bankrupt in the NHL since World War II.

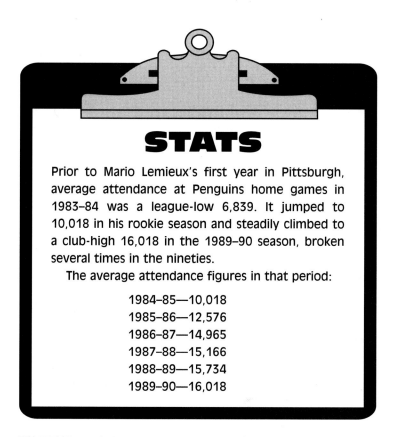

STATS

Prior to Mario Lemieux's first year in Pittsburgh, average attendance at Penguins home games in 1983–84 was a league-low 6,839. It jumped to 10,018 in his rookie season and steadily climbed to a club-high 16,018 in the 1989–90 season, broken several times in the nineties.

The average attendance figures in that period:

1984–85—10,018
1985–86—12,576
1986–87—14,965
1987–88—15,166
1988–89—15,734
1989–90—16,018

Even after finding new investors and new money, the Penguins had the same old problems on the ice. They hit rock bottom in the standings in 1983–84 when they had their worst record in history at 16–58–6. Fans continued to stay away and the team continued to lose money.

Finishing last had its rewards, however. The team that finishes last in the NHL has the No. 1 pick in the amateur player draft following the season. Mario Lemieux was at the top of the Penguins' list, as he was for every other team in the NHL.

Lemieux was billed as the next Gretzky—a heavy responsibility to put on the shoulders of a mere eighteen-year-old. Lemieux wore number 66 on his uniform as an upside-down tribute to the Great One's trademark 99. It was unfair, of course, to compare such a young player with the greatest player in the game. But the message was clear: Like Gretzky, Lemieux was a player who could carry a team.

In this case, Lemieux was expected not only to carry the Penguins on the ice but to help solve their financial problems as well. There were rumblings that the lack of fan support would force the cash-strapped Penguins to leave town.

In practice, Lemieux had showed his teammates his skills against the Penguins' own defense. But how would he perform against the NHL's best once the season actually started?

Opening night at Boston Garden against the Boston Bruins on October 11, 1984, presented Lemieux with a problem. The historic Garden was the NHL's oldest arena. It featured a small ice surface that favored the close-checking Bruins. Lemieux preferred a larger rink, which was better suited to his open-ice skating abilities. This was going to be a tough place for a rookie to start.

The Bruins featured All-Star defenseman Ray Bourque. Boston had tied for the second-best record in the league the year before. Early in the game, Bourque had the puck on his stick. Whenever Bourque had the puck, the crowd expected something to happen. Something did. Mario Lemieux, the Penguins' rookie, snatched the puck off Bourque's stick, skated around him, and roared down ice toward the Boston goal.

With the ease of his days in junior hockey, Lemieux faked goaltender Pete Peeters to his knees. He flipped the puck past Peeters for a goal with less than three minutes gone in the game. The play had come on Lemieux's first shift in the NHL. And he had beaten one of the league's great defensemen to do it.

On opening night in Pittsburgh, a spirited crowd

Mario Lemieux's first goal in the NHL came on his first shift and his first shot, as he fired the puck past Boston Bruins' goaltender Pete Peeters.

of 15,741 filled the Civic Arena known unofficially as the "Igloo." The average attendance the year before had been only 6,839. In tribute to Mario Lemieux, fans brought their own signs: "We love 66."

And Mario Lemieux loved Pittsburgh, a western Pennsylvania town known as the Steel City, with a history tied to the steel industry. "Pittsburgh is so much different than Montreal," Lemieux said. "Montreal is a big, big city. Here you can walk the street at night and nobody bothers you."[2]

Because Lemieux was so young, and in order to ease his transition into his new culture, the Penguins placed him with the Matthews family of Mt. Lebanon, Pennsylvania. The Matthews clan became Lemieux's extended family. Lemieux's life had totally changed. Before, he had always shared a bedroom with his brother Richard. Now he was alone in his own bedroom. However, he had new friends to compete against in video games—one of his favorite hobbies. The Matthews family had three sons.

In the middle of the day, Lemieux could be found sitting in front of a television set. He was not watching sports. He was watching a soap opera. Lemieux had never mastered the English language, and the soap operas helped him improve his language skills—somewhat.

One day, he was being interviewed by a popular Pittsburgh radio talk show host with a strong local accent. Lemieux later admitted he had not understood a word the interviewer had said. "I just answered the questions, 'Yes . . . no . . . I think so.'"[3]

Talking to the press, though, was a responsibility that Lemieux did not always enjoy. "I used to run into the bathroom after games so I wouldn't have to talk to reporters," Lemieux said.[4]

After games at the Igloo, Lemieux was besieged by autograph seekers. Lemieux patiently signed every autograph requested as he worked his way through the crowd toward his truck.

The next stop for Lemieux was the NHL All-Star Game. It was a showcase for the greatest players in hockey. Wayne Gretzky, Marcel Dionne, and Mike Bossy were all playing. "I didn't expect to be here at all," Lemieux said. "There are so many good players in our division."[5]

Some critics believed that Lemieux did not belong. Despite his impressive record—he was leading all rookies in scoring at the All-Star break with 60 points, counting goals and assists—it was felt he did not put out full effort. The reputation was partly built on the fact that he hated team practices. He never trained with weights and seemed to "loaf" on the ice. Lemieux's long strides

A frightening sight for any goaltender: Mario Lemieux skates in front of the net with the puck.

and effortless-looking style of skating gave the impression he was not working hard. One of his biggest critics was Don Cherry, a colorful television commentator. He had called Lemieux "the biggest floater in the NHL."

"It hurts a little bit," Lemieux said of Cherry's comments, which came right before the NHL All-Star Game.[6]

The game was tied, 2–2, between Lemieux's Wales Conference team and Gretzky's Campbell Conference team midway through the second period. Then Lemieux went to work. Anders Hedberg charged to the slot area in front of the net where Lemieux found him with a perfect pass. Hedberg drove the puck past goaltender Grant Fuhr. With Lemieux's assist, the Wales Conference was now leading 3–2.

It was the kind of wide-open game that Lemieux loved. There was plenty of skating and no hitting. Lemieux, surging with newfound confidence, accelerated the pace.

Four minutes later, Lemieux teamed with Bourque and Kirk Muller on a three-way passing play. Lemieux capped the play when he ripped a shot from ten feet out to beat Fuhr for his first goal of the game. Fans at the Calgary Saddledome in Calgary, Alberta, Canada, roared their approval.

Gretzky scored midway through the third period to pull the Campbell Conference within one goal. The Wales' lead was now down to 4–3. One minute later, Lemieux took a pass from Bourque at the red line. Lemieux raced past the defense, cut into the middle, and scored to give the Wales a 5–3 lead and its eventual winning goal. The final score was Wales 6, Campbell 4. Lemieux earned the most valuable player award. "Winning the All-Star Game MVP gave him the confidence that he belonged," Penguins general manager Eddie Johnston said.[7]

Lemieux was the best thing to happen to Penguins hockey. Attendance was up over three thousand people per game. The Penguins' victory total was up too. They won eight more games than they had the previous season. But despite the presence of Lemieux in the 1984–85 season, the Penguins simply were not strong enough to compete with better teams in the NHL. However, there was still one race that was going strong toward the end of the season—the battle for rookie of the year.

Despite missing seven games, Lemieux had scored 100 points on 43 goals and 57 assists. This was the third highest total-points scored for a rookie in NHL history. But the competition for the Calder Trophy was intense. Chris Chelios of the Montreal Canadiens, one of the top young defensemen in the

FACT

Mario Lemieux scored a goal in his first game, on his first shift, and on his first shot in the NHL. Other highlights of his rookie season:

- Lemieux became only the third rookie in NHL history to score at least 100 points. He holds the Penguins' rookie records for most goals (43), assists (57), and points (100).

- He was selected as the NHL's Rookie of the Year and was named to the NHL All-Rookie team.

- He was named Most Valuable Player at the All-Star Game.

league, was also in the running. Finally, the voters felt that Lemieux's accomplishments were more spectacular, and he won rookie of the year.

Tom McMillan, who covered the Penguins for the *Pittsburgh Post-Gazette*, said of Lemieux:

> He was the absolute focus of every team's game plan. There was no one here to take the heat off him. I'll never forget that year: different language, different culture, horrible team, and all the pressure of people. He was a one man show.[8]

Chapter 5

World Champion

The scene was the World Hockey Championship in Prague, Czechoslovakia, in 1985. The opponent for the Canadian team was the powerful Soviet Union hockey team. Mario Lemieux had performed well in his first year in the NHL. But his history in international competition had been less than glittering—when he decided to play. He had been criticized for a lack of patriotism for rejecting a number of previous invitations to play for Team Canada. However, in the spring of 1985, Lemieux was playing at the world championships as if he meant to create a new image for himself.

Lemieux faced Viacheslav Fetisov, the Soviet's top defenseman and one of the best in the world. Controlling the puck, Fetisov came steaming down the ice. He looked for an open teammate to receive his pass. Suddenly, there was Lemieux facing him.

Fetisov swerved abruptly, losing control of the puck. Before the great defenseman could recover, Lemieux swept the puck onto his stick and headed for the Soviet goal. There were defenders behind him and open ice ahead of him. Lemieux streaked into Soviet territory. Guarding the net was goaltender Vladimir Myshkin. He tensed, waiting for Lemieux's shot. Lemieux snapped the puck past Myshkin's outstretched glove for the score. It was now 3–0 Canada—too late for the Soviets to come back. Lemieux's second goal of the game had clinched an upset victory for Canada over the Soviets.

Canada's own try for the gold was thwarted by home-team Czechoslovakia in the finals. Lemieux and his teammates had to settle for the second-place silver medal. Silver was nice, but only gold would suffice for Lemieux. Wasn't the point of playing hockey to win championships? Two years later, Lemieux again had the opportunity to do just that at the 1987 Canada Cup tournament.

Described as the unofficial world championship, the Canada Cup was played every few years on an irregular basis before the start of the NHL season. The World Hockey Championships were played during the Stanley Cup playoffs. But everyone was available for the Canada Cup. The wider range of NHL players made it a truer measure of greatness. Few rivalries were greater than the one between Canada and the Soviet Union.

Two of the world's great hockey powers had waged some fierce battles at various levels. None was greater, however, than the so-called Summit Series. Back in 1972 the NHL's best challenged the Soviet's best in a knock-down, drag-out eight-game series that stretched from Montreal to Moscow. After seven games, the series was tied at three games apiece with one tie. The final game in Moscow would prove which hockey giant was better. Finally, Paul Henderson scored with just 34 seconds left in regulation to give the Canadians the heart-stopping decisive game in the fiercely competitive, hard-hitting series. It was widely regarded as the most famous goal in Canadian hockey history.

FACT

With Mario Lemieux in the lineup, the Penguins' regular-season record during his career was 367–312–66. Without him: 96–101–30.

Now Mario Lemieux was trying to make his own history at the 1987 Canada Cup. Lemieux seemed bent on a one-man crusade. He scored three goals in Canada's 3–2 victory over the United States. He also blasted his critics. "Where are they now?" he asked.[1] He was enjoying every minute of his first Canada Cup experience.

Lemieux added two more goals in the

Canadians' 5–3 victory over Czechoslovakia. Memories flooded back from the world championships when the Canadians had lost to the Czechs. It was sweet revenge.

The victory catapulted the Canadians into the best-of-three championship series against their old adversaries, the Soviets. In Game 1, the Soviets threw a tight defensive net around Lemieux. The frustrated Lemieux, who had been leading the tournament with seven goals, was not able to score. The result was a 6–5 overtime victory for the Soviets.

Now the Canadians were in a must-win situation. A loss in Game 2 meant the Soviets would take the gold medal. The Canadians had to win two in a row from the powerful Soviet team to win the Cup. It was not going to be easy. A string of injuries had knocked out many of Canada's top forwards.

"When we lost the players, then we had to come up with something different in terms of combinations that would generate more offense for us," Team Canada coach Mike Keenan said. "Sometimes you do things you don't know why you do them. But you just do them."[2]

What Mike Keenan did was the most improbable of all—he put Mario Lemieux and Wayne Gretzky, both centers, on the same line for Game 2. Lemieux played out of position on the right wing. Until that

Lemieux (right) shadows Wayne Gretzky (left) early in Lemieux's career. They would later line up on the same side for Team Canada.

point, the two had played on separate lines. Usually the only time they were on the ice together was when the Canadians had a power play. Imagine having Lemieux and Gretzky on the ice while your team is skating with a one-man or two-man advantage, which is what happens during power-play time. A team is rewarded with such an advantage when its opponent is penalized for an infraction.

The Canadian team rushed to a 3–1 lead, only to have the Soviets come back and tie 3–3 in the second period. Once again, Lemieux was being held scoreless. With less than four minutes left in the second period, Lemieux and Gretzky teamed up on a classic two-on-one play. The pair had broken loose with only one Soviet defenseman between them and the goal.

Gretzky skated down the left side. He feathered a cross-ice pass to Lemieux, and the big man beat Soviet goaltender Evgeny Belosheikin for a goal at 16:32. The Soviets came back to tie the game. Then Lemieux and Gretzky teamed up for a 5–4 lead, Canada.

All of Canada was about to celebrate. Victory looked certain. But with just 64 seconds left, the Soviets tied the game again. The teams went into overtime, tied 5–5. In the locker room, the Game 1 loss to the Soviets dominated everyone's thoughts.

It seemed to be happening again. Canada had also had a 5–4 lead in the first game. The Soviets had tied it late in the third period before winning in overtime. "We had to relax and not panic," Lemieux said. "We had to keep our concentration."[3]

The Canadian team battled the mighty Soviets blow for a blow like two great heavyweight fighters slugging it out in the ring. Both sides had chances to score, but were turned away time and again. Soviet goaltender Evgeny Belosheikin and Canadian goaltender Grant Fuhr kept topping each other with spectacular saves. The teams went back to the dressing room after a scoreless overtime period. Then they skated back on the ice for another period.

"I said, this is crazy, what's going on here?" noted Team Canada defenseman Paul Coffey. "We had chances, they had chances. . . ."[4]

The game was going into its fourth hour. Everyone was tired and running on adrenaline. At 10:07 of the second overtime, the winning goal was scored. The players were battling for the puck in a wild scramble in front of the net.

Gretzky caught the puck on his stick and lashed a shot at the Soviet goal. The Soviet goaltender stopped the shot. No goal. But the puck had rebounded. Lemieux swept the rebound into the open side.

The dramatic goal gave Canada a 6–5 victory and touched off thunderous uproar from the more than seventeen thousand fans. The series went into a deciding third game.

Gretzky had assisted on all three goals by Lemieux. Could they perform their magic one more time? With less than two minutes left in regulation in Game 3, the teams were tied 5–5. They set up for a faceoff in the Canadian zone. Canada's Dale Hawerchuk won and pushed the puck to Lemieux. Lemieux passed ahead to Gretzky at center ice. The Canadian team rushed into the Soviet zone on a three-on-one breakaway. Gretzky carried the puck over the blue line. He looked around the ice and saw Larry Murphy and Mario Lemieux coming down hard. "I saw No. 66 [Lemieux] and that's where the puck was going," Gretzky said, "there was no doubt about that."[5] Gretzky put the puck on Lemieux's stick. Lemieux then put it where Soviet goaltender Sergei Mylnikov could not reach it, high in the net, for his tournament-leading eleventh goal.

The score was 6–5, Canada. There was 1:26 left in the game. This was more than enough time for a Soviet comeback. It had happened before. Lemieux was aware of that. "We had to stay calm after the goal," he said. "We only had a little time left and we didn't want to get caught and scored against."[6]

As the final buzzer went off, signaling Canada's 6–5 triumph, players jumped on the ice to celebrate. The crowd was celebrating, too. They had applauded and roared throughout the exciting contest. Now the din in the Copps Coliseum had reached a new level.

The 1987 Canada Cup would be one for the ages. It could only be fully appreciated when put into historical perspective years later, much like the great Summit Series of 1972. Like Paul Henderson, who had scored the memorable goal against the Soviets fifteen years before, Lemieux too became a national folk hero in Canada.

He was already a local folk hero in Pittsburgh. He had lifted the level of the Penguins' play through the 1980s. But could he lift them to a championship, as he had for Team Canada?

FACT

How important was Mario Lemieux to the Pittsburgh Penguins? Consider that he was involved in the scoring in roughly half their goals during his career.

- During his twelve seasons in Pittsburgh, Mario Lemieux recorded a point (goal or assist) on 1,494 of the Penguins' 3,064 goals (48.8 percent).

- Lemieux was on the ice for 1,886 of the team's 3,064 goals (61.6 percent).

- He had a point in 639 of his 745 career games (85.8 percent) and two or more points in 432 games (58.1 percent.)

Chapter 6

A Star Among Stars

Mario Lemieux was bursting with confidence following Team Canada's victory. He had scored the goal that conquered the Soviets. An entire country was proclaiming him a hero. With a sweep of his hockey stick, he had swept away all negative impressions.

Playing with other great talents against the world's best, Lemieux had learned what it took to compete on the highest level and to be a winner. With the Penguins failing to make the playoffs in Lemieux's first three years, he had few high-pressure challenges. The Canada Cup had been a turning point in his career.

In the 1987–88 season, Lemieux was off to the best start of his career. In addition, the Penguins had acquired Paul Coffey, a dazzling defenseman who had played with Lemieux in the Canada Cup. It gave them a powerful one-two punch. Coffey was regarded as the best skating defenseman in the league. He was a brilliant passer and scorer who would be a perfect complement to Lemieux.

". . . Mario is so good with the puck, mostly from center ice in," Coffey said. "If you get a guy like myself who can move the puck up to him quick, it takes an enormous amount of pressure off him."[1]

The results began to show. Just past the midpoint of the season, Lemieux had already scored 52 goals. This was a figure most players would be happy to have over an entire year. Lemieux's league-leading 114 total points was just 27 shy of his all-time best season. It made him a clear choice for the All-Star Game in St. Louis. He had really turned up his intensity.

At the 1988 All-Star Game, Lemieux started for the Wales Conference. Across the ice was his Canada Cup partner, Wayne Gretzky. He was now his opponent, playing for the Campbell Conference.

In the 1983 All-Star Game at Uniondale, New York, Gretzky had set a record with four goals in the midseason classic and tied another with his four points. The Edmonton Oilers' star had become only the second player in All-Star history to score three or more goals in a game.

The All-Star Game had been a showcase for Gretzky. Now it was Lemieux versus Gretzky. Gretzky scored a goal to give his team a 2–1 lead in the first period. But by the midpoint of the second period, Lemieux's team was winning 3–2. In a one-man show, Lemieux had set up all three goals for his team.

FACT

Before Mario Lemieux came to Pittsburgh, the Penguins had the worst record in the NHL in 1983–84. Here is a look at the Penguins' record the year before Lemieux's arrival and their record through their first playoff appearance with him in 1989:

Season	W	L	T	Points	Finish
1983–84	16	58	6	38	21st
1984–85	24	51	5	53	20th
1985–86	34	38	8	76	15th
1986–87	30	38	12	72	14th
1987–88	36	35	9	81	12th
1988–89	40	33	7	87	6th

Now Lemieux had the puck behind the goal line. Using all his strength, he muscled his way around the net and shot. Goaltender Mike Vernon stopped Lemieux's first attempt, but the Penguins' star stretched out his long frame. Corralling the rebound on his stick, he quickly flicked a shot into the net before the stunned Vernon could react.

"He has such long arms," Vernon said. Lemieux's goal had made the score 4–2. "He reached around far behind the net. We'll see that goal (in highlight films) several times the rest of the season, I'm sure."[2]

With the score tied, 4–4, in the third period, Lemieux took a setup pass from Mats Naslund and waited. When Vernon dropped down to block the shot, Lemieux lifted the puck over the goaltender for the score. Lemieux had simply outmaneuvered and outwitted the goaltender.

"You never have any idea what to expect," Philadelphia goaltender Dominic Roussel said of Lemieux. "His face is so calm. He shows no sign of stress or anything. A lot of goaltenders get nervous when he's coming at them with that face. It's as if he's saying, 'No problem. Relax. I'm just going to beat you now. It's not going to hurt a bit.'"[3]

Lemieux had already scored a record-breaking five points and was still going strong. So was

It was hats off to Mario Lemieux after he was awarded the MVP trophy (and the pickup truck that went along with it) at the 1988 All-Star Game in St. Louis.

Gretzky's Campbell Conference team. Suddenly, it was a tie game, 5–5, that went into overtime.

The combination of Lemieux and Naslund had worked wonders earlier in the game. Now Naslund again passed the puck to Lemieux in front of the net. Lemieux faked the goaltender to the side. The goaltender crashed down to stop the puck. Lemieux slipped the puck back toward the middle of Vernon's legs, where there was an opening. At 1:08 into overtime, Lemieux had scored the winning goal.

Naslund's assist on the tie-breaking goal was his fifth of the game. It was an All-Star record, but not for long. It was overshadowed by Lemieux's six-point All-Star Game record. Lemieux was voted MVP of the All-Star Game for the second time in his career.

Lemieux was about to move in on Gretzky's territory. For seven straight years, Gretzky had won the NHL scoring title. For eight straight years, he had been voted most valuable player. Now there was a new man on the scene. Lemieux was the winner in both categories in the 1987–88 season.

To reach 50 goals in an NHL season was considered quite an accomplishment. To score 60 was rare. Lemieux scored 70 goals. This was a figure exceeded at that point by only three players in NHL

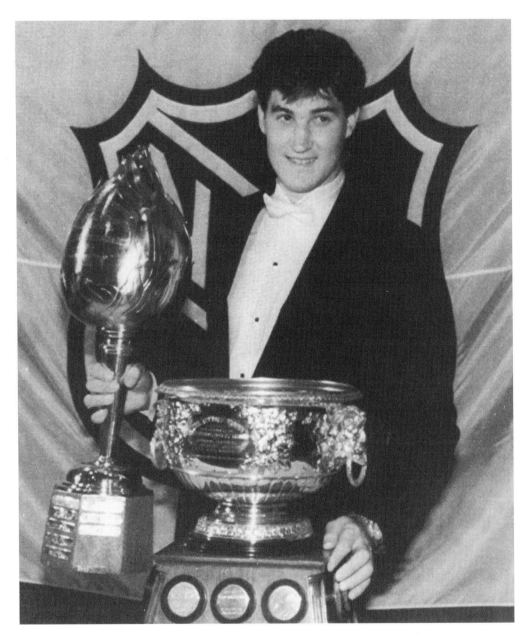

Lemieux was the NHL's Most Valuable Player and scoring champion in the 1987–88 season, when he scored a league-leading 70 goals.

history. Gretzky had surpassed that figure on four occasions, including an astounding 92 goals in 1981–82.

Despite Lemieux's extraordinary season, the Penguins once again failed to make the playoffs. Obviously, they needed more help. The Penguins acquired Tom Barrasso, the award-winning goalie, in a trade with the Buffalo Sabres. Barrasso had been the NHL rookie of the year. He had won the Vezina Trophy for best goaltender and had also been an All-Star. Another new player, left wing Kevin Stevens, whom the Penguins picked up in a deal with Los Angeles, was on the brink of stardom.

The Penguins were ready to go on the attack. Leading the way was Mario Lemieux. In the 1988–89 season, Lemieux scored a career-high 85 goals. Five came in one game against the New Jersey Devils, when Lemieux scored in every way possible. He scored:

- A power-play goal. (A team is given a one-man or two-man advantage when the other team commits an infraction).

- Short-handed. (Skating with one or two players less because of a penalty.)

- Into an empty net. (The opposing goaltender is no longer guarding the net. He has been taken off the ice and replaced with an extra skater. This usually occurs late in the game when a team is losing by one goal.)

- On a penalty shot. (The most exciting play in hockey. Skater versus goaltender. A skater comes in from center ice and tries to beat the goaltender one-on-one. This shot is only awarded to a team when the referee thinks a player has been illegally prevented from an apparent goal-scoring opportunity. Lemieux was considered the best in the league at the penalty shot because of his long reach and ability to control the puck.)

- Even-strength. (Both sides are skating with a full complement of players.)

During that season, hockey fans not only saw Lemieux pulling off miracles, but also saw another kind of miracle: the Penguins in the playoffs. For the first time in seven years, they found themselves in the postseason tournament. Their first-round opponent was the New York Rangers. The Penguins quickly disposed of them in four straight games.

Next up was the Philadelphia Flyers. Lemieux was subpar in the first four games. He was hurt in a midice collision. He had strained his neck so that any motion was extremely painful. Continuing to play in pain, Lemieux scored five goals in Game 5.

FACT

Mario Lemieux's five favorite goal-scoring targets:

1. John Vanbiesbrouck, 30
2. Empty net, 28
3. Ron Hextall, 19
4. and 5. (tied) Pete Peeters and Don Beaupre, 15

Still, the Penguins were eventually eliminated by the Flyers.

What happened next was the talk of the hockey world. From the start of the 1989–90 season, Lemieux was on fire. Game after game, he had a hand in the Penguins' scoring. His back was on fire, too. Lemieux felt searing pain that was so intense, it sometimes prevented him from bending over. "Most players wouldn't even have bothered to suit up because of the pain," said teammate John Cullen.[4]

FACT

Mario Lemieux scored more points (122) against the New Jersey Devils than he scored against any other team in the NHL. He played 60 games against the Devils in his career. Here are his statistics against other teams in his top five:

Team	Games Played	Points
New York Rangers	61	119
New York Islanders	59	116
Philadelphia	60	104
Washington	55	92

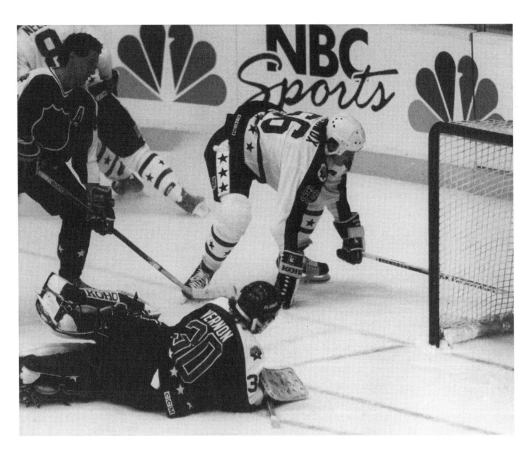

Lemieux was the star once again, as he scored his third goal for the Wales Conference in the 1990 All-Star Game in Pittsburgh, helping his team to a 12–7 victory.

Pain or no pain, Lemieux could not quit. He was on a streak—one of the longest in hockey history. By the middle of February, Lemieux had either scored a goal or assisted on one for forty-six straight games. That did not include the All-Star Game in Pittsburgh when Lemieux scored a record-tying 4 goals to walk off with his third MVP award in the event. Now he was five games away from Gretzky's all-time record of 51. As he got closer to the record, each game became increasingly more difficult. Many times, drawn and pale, Lemieux greeted reporters after games wearing a brace strapped around his midsection. "It gets tougher and tougher to play back-to-back games," Lemieux said. "It is getting worse as it goes along. I don't think I would have played if it wasn't for the streak. But, unfortunately, I can't take a night off at this point."[5]

It was February 14, 1990, and the Penguins' opponent was the New York Rangers. The place was Madison Square Garden. Lemieux's back had been unusually troublesome, but he was not about to let it get in the way of his dreams. During the first period, he tried to take a regular shift. It was too tough and he ended up back on the bench.

He tried to play the power plays in the second period, but he did not have the strength for it. The pain was overwhelming and he went back on the bench. Tears streamed down his face. He just said, "I can't help the team." Lemieux and the streak were both finished.[6] Very little was said on the bench. Coach Craig Patrick told the team to "go out and win it for Mario."[7] They did.

Chapter 7

Bound for Glory

Perspiration broke out on his forehead and dripped down his face. Kneeling on one knee, the assistant equipment manager of the Pittsburgh Penguins was intensely concentrating on getting the laces tied just right. The stakes were high. He was tying the laces of the greatest hockey player in the world. There was pressure to do it just right. Mario Lemieux looked down and smiled. "I don't ever remember sweating like that when I tied my own laces."[1]

Every move Lemieux made, he had to be careful. Bending could cause his back to go out of whack. Almost without warning, his back would act up and suddenly, no Mario on the ice. And no way of knowing how long he would be gone.

Doctors discovered a herniated disk in Lemieux's lower back. He had played through the pain in the 1989–90 season. He knew he should rest his back, but he couldn't. Not if he wanted to help the team. He fell short of breaking Wayne Gretzky's record scoring streak only when the pain became impossible. His back pain forced him to miss twenty-one games.

"There were lots of nights that I tossed and turned in bed and couldn't even sleep because I would feel a sharp pain running up and down my spine," Lemieux said.[2]

Finally, it was decided. Lemieux would undergo surgery in the summer of 1990 to correct the problem. The operation was a success, but the pain continued, worse than ever. Doctors were puzzled until they discovered a rare bone infection in Lemieux's lower back. He would need continuous doses of antibiotics and plenty of rest. "I had some doubts that I would ever play the game," Lemieux said.[3]

By the third week of December doctors had Lemieux on a light workout program: stretching, swimming, and riding a stationary bike. He was determined to get back, and he spared no sweat to do it. On December 30, Lemieux resumed light skating. He was just happy to be working out with his teammates again.

"Just seeing his equipment hanging in his locker is a great sign," defenseman Paul Coffey said.[4] Lemieux was now pain-free, but was he in game shape? That would only be determined once Lemieux hit the ice against a hard-hitting NHL opponent. Skating with teammates was certainly no substitute for full-scale competition.

Lemieux had missed fifty games of the 1990–91 season. When he stepped on the ice for his first game against the Quebec Nordiques, he was quickly thrust into the violent world of the NHL. Early in the game, Lemieux was hammered to the ice by a solid check from Nordiques forward Paul Gillis. Lemieux scrambled to his feet and continued playing.

It was not until the second period that he started to show flashes of his old self. His crisp passes found teammates' sticks in scoring position, and they put the puck in the net. Before you could say Le Magnifique (Mario's nickname in French, meaning "The Magnificent One"), he had three assists and the Penguins had a 6–5 victory.

It had been a good show by Lemieux. It was certainly more than anyone expected in his first NHL game in nearly ten months. For Lemieux, it had

After taking time off to rest his injured back, Mario Lemieux was eager to return to the ice and help his team once again.

extra-special meaning. His friends and family were at the game, which was played in his native province.

"I think I looked pretty bad in the first (period)," Lemieux said. "I was thinking about being checked, especially from behind, and I didn't want to put myself in that position. But in the second and third period, I felt a lot better and made better plays."[5]

Lemieux's return had sparked an already potent Pittsburgh team. It featured several young players—Jaromir Jagr, Kevin Stevens, and Mark Recchi—who were coming of age. The Penguins boasted one of the league's top goaltenders in Tom Barrasso. It also had a strong group of veterans that included Paul Coffey, Bryan Trottier, Joe Mullen, and Larry Murphy. The Penguins, however, believed they still needed some missing pieces if they were to compete in the playoffs. The team got those missing pieces in a six-player trade with Hartford when they acquired Ron Francis, one of the NHL's top two-way (checking and scoring) forwards, and Ulf Samuelsson, one of the NHL's most rugged defensemen.

The Penguins believed they now had a tougher team to withstand the rigors of the playoffs. They found instant chemistry with their new additions. Led by Lemieux, the Penguins soared through the Patrick Division. Even though Lemieux played only

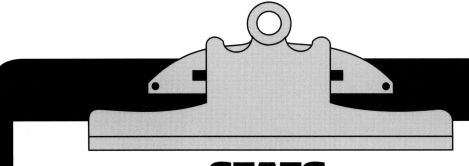

STATS

Mario Lemieux's base salary of $11,321,429 in the 1996–97 season was more than the combined total of the next two players behind him (Mark Messier, $6,000,000, and Wayne Gretzky, $5,047,500, both of the New York Rangers).

The top ten in the NHL salary structure:

1.	Mario Lemieux, Pittsburgh	$11,321,429
2.	Mark Messier, New York Rangers	$6,000,000
3.	Wayne Gretzky, New York Rangers	$5,047,500
4.	Pavel Bure, Vancouver	$5,000,000
5.	Pat LaFontaine, Buffalo	$4,600,000
6.	Patrick Roy, Colorado	$4,455,944
7.	Brett Hull, St. Louis	$4,400,000
8. and 9. (tied)	Sergei Fedorov, Detroit, and Dominik Hasek, Buffalo	$4,200,000
10.	Eric Lindros, Philadelphia	$4,182,000

one fourth of the season, he made an impact. He managed to rank fifth on the team in scoring. He was an inspiration to his teammates. By the end of the season, the Penguins were first in their division—the first championship of any kind in their history. But the regular season was just a warm-up for the much rougher playoffs. Could Lemieux's fragile back stand up to the punishment of playoff hockey where there was tighter checking and more intense physical play?

Despite finishing with their best record in history, the Penguins were still considered a long shot to win the Stanley Cup. Six teams in the league had better records. When the playoffs began, the Penguins' first-round opponent was the New Jersey Devils. The Penguins lost three of the first five games and were one game away from elimination. They had to win in New Jersey in order to stay alive. They did, 4–3. They brought the series back to Pittsburgh and beat the Devils 4–0 to clinch the first-round series, four games to three.

Next up were the Washington Capitals. Once again, the Penguins lost the opener. Once again, they battled back to win the series—this time winning four straight.

The Boston Bruins were next. The Penguins lost the first game. The Penguins lost the second game.

Now their fans were worried. The Penguins had an awesome task in front of them. They had to win four out of the next five games against the Bruins, a team that had finished twelve points ahead of them in the conference standings. The Penguins had had no luck against Boston in previous years, losing to them both times they met in the playoffs.

The Penguins were desperate for a victory. When they got two wins, the series was tied and it went back to Boston. The Penguins had won only seven times in twenty-four years in Boston. However, they won this time, and led the series, 3–2. Another victory in Pittsburgh clinched the conference title for the Penguins.

The Penguins were in the Stanley Cup finals for the first time in their history. As captain, Lemieux was the first to carry the Prince of Wales Trophy around the ice. He had already been carrying the team with a playoff-leading 32 points so far. His back had stood up to the physical punishment of playoff hockey.

"To see that big guy carrying the [Prince of Wales Trophy] cup around the ice brought a tear to your eye. He probably saved hockey in this town," said Penguins forward Phil Bourque.[6]

The Pittsburgh Penguins and the Stanley Cup finals. Those two were not normally said in the same sentence. However, in their twenty-fourth year in the NHL, the Penguins had finally advanced to hockey's biggest show, thanks in large part to Lemieux.

He had been sidelined for nearly a year with his back problems. He had missed fifty games of the 1990–91 season, before returning late in the year. He had complained of fatigue early in the New Jersey series. Yet he still managed to lead the Penguins' charge into the finals with 11 goals and

FACT

Mario Lemieux is the only player in NHL history to have won all of the following trophies: the Ross (NHL scoring championship), Hart (the league's most valuable player), Pearson (NHL's outstanding player, as selected by the players' association), Calder (rookie of the year), Smythe (playoff MVP), Masterton (the player who best exemplifies the qualities of perseverance, sportsmanship, and dedication to hockey), and All-Star Game MVP.

Here is a list of his honors and awards:

The Hart in 1988, 1993, and 1996
The Smythe in 1991 and 1992
NHL All-Star Game MVP in 1985, 1988, and 1990
The Ross in 1988, 1989, 1992, 1993, 1996, and 1997
The Calder in 1985
The Masterton in 1993
The Pearson in 1986, 1988, 1993, and 1996

21 assists in eighteen playoff games. "You can see the determination on Mario's face," linemate Mark Recchi said. "He's been unbelievable. He's doing it all because he wants to win so badly."[7]

Lemieux continued his offensive surge with a short-handed goal against the Minnesota North Stars in the first game of the Stanley Cup finals. But the Penguins continued their habit of losing the opening game.

Game 2 boasted a play that alone was worth the price of admission. Lemieux was carrying the puck up ice when he was confronted by Minnesota defenseman Shawn Chambers. Lemieux faked to his right, then cut inside. He backhanded the puck between Chambers's legs, skated around him, and picked it up with his forehand. Now he was breaking into the clear and roaring in on Jon Casey. It was a frightening sight for the Minnesota goaltender.

Casey would let Mario make the first move. It did not help. Lemieux switched the puck from his forehand to his backhand. Casey was faked out and Lemieux, while sliding to his knees, put the puck into a wide-open net.

The Pittsburgh players had seen their illustrious teammate doing miraculous things since returning from his serious back ailment. This topped them all. But their elation following a 4–1 victory in Game 2

A typical sight during the 1991 Stanley Cup Finals: Mario Lemieux scores a goal against the Minnesota North Stars.

quickly turned to deflation. Lemieux was suffering from back spasms and would not be able to play when the series resumed with Game 3 in Minnesota. Without their big man, the Penguins lost 3–1 and fell behind two games to one in the best-of-seven series.

An air of mystery surrounded Lemieux. When the Penguins held their off-day press conference, there was no Lemieux. In fact, there were no Pittsburgh players at all. Only coach Bob Johnson and general manager (GM) Craig Patrick showed up for a scheduled media session. Johnson and Patrick had to face the barrage of an angry press. Where were the players? Particularly, where was Lemieux?

The coach and GM had no answers. Their only response was that Lemieux was "resting" and it was still up in the air whether he would play the next day. It seemed that decision would be made right before game time. When the players came out for the pregame skate, Lemieux was with them. Floating around the ice, he seemed to show no after-effects of his back ailment.

The game started and Lemieux took his first shift. All doubts were soon erased as he plunged right into the play. Lemieux was all over the ice, beating the North Stars to the puck, and dealing out ferocious hits. He fired a goal-mouth pass to Recchi to set up a score 2:58 into the game. By that time, the

Penguins had built a three-goal lead and were on their way to a 5–3 victory. The series was tied 2–2. It was back to Pittsburgh for Game 5.

Lemieux was out of control. Out of the North Stars' control, that is. The Penguins were on the offense in the first period when Murphy shot wide of the net. Lemieux picked up the rebound and skated in front. He switched from backhand to forehand, then swept the puck past Casey. He set up two other goals in a four-goal first period. The final score was Pittsburgh 6, Minnesota 4.

The Penguins were now one game away from the Stanley Cup championship. Lemieux seemed to be a player on a mission. His back problems seemed to be just a memory. He was in such a state of concentration that nothing bothered him. Players who are thus locked into a higher concentration are said to be in a "zone." Everything Lemieux touched seemed to turn to goals for the Penguins.

In Game 6, the Penguins took a 1–0 lead, but suddenly found themselves in a hole when they committed two straight penalties. This forced the Penguins to skate short-handed. Two of their players had to sit in the penalty box for two minutes each.

The Penguins would skate with only three players against the North Stars' five during the concurrent penalties. It was a big advantage for

FACT

Following the 1997 Stanley Cup playoffs, Lemieux had the highest goals-per-game-average in NHL playoff history (.787) with 70 in 89 games.

Minnesota. Lemieux was sent on the ice as one of the "penalty killers." He was one of the best in the league at that job. With his long reach and towering figure, Lemieux covered the ice like a blanket. He swept his stick back and forth across the ice, interrupting the other team's flow. He was a dangerous offensive threat as well. He was someone who could quickly turn a short-handed disadvantage into a short-handed goal.

No sooner had Lemieux deflected one of the North Stars' passes than he was the victim of a Minnesota penalty. The result was that the Penguins were now skating only one man short. Moments later, Lemieux intercepted a Minnesota pass and was headed in the other direction with the puck. Before the North Stars realized it, Lemieux had scored a short-handed goal to put Pittsburgh up 2–0. He added three assists as the Penguins crushed the North Stars 8–0 for their first Stanley Cup championship.

"It seemed like anything that was within 20 feet he reached," Minnesota's Dave Gagner said of Lemieux. "When somebody that big and that good wants to win that badly, there isn't much you can do."[8]

Lemieux had scored five goals and assisted on seven others in the finals, despite sitting out one of

With great pride, Mario Lemieux holds the Stanley Cup over his head after leading the Pittsburgh Penguins to victory in 1991.

In both 1991 and 1992, Lemieux was awarded the Smythe Trophy, as Most Valuable Player of the Stanley Cup playoffs.

the six games with back spasms. His spectacular performance earned him the Most Valuable Player trophy in the playoffs. But it was the Stanley Cup trophy that was closest to his heart. It was his only goal when he came to Pittsburgh. He lifted the Cup high over his head in the traditional postgame skate around the ice. It was appropriate. After all, Lemieux had almost single-handedly lifted the Penguins to their first league championship.

Chapter 8

Beating the Odds

It was a cold day in January 1993. The news hit Lemieux harder than any blindside check he had taken in an NHL game. It had been such a small lump on his neck. The doctors diagnosed Hodgkin's disease, a form of cancer that attacks the lymph nodes.

"That certainly was the toughest day of my life," Lemieux remembered. "When the doctors gave me the news, (I was) crying the whole day."[1] How could he tell his girlfriend, Nathalie Asselin, who was pregnant with their first child? Lemieux was going to be a father, but would he live long enough to be able to see his child grow up?

The moment Nathalie saw Mario, she knew something was terribly wrong. But what? What could possibly be causing such agony? Mario could hardly get the words out. It took him an hour before he could tell her. Telling his parents was even more difficult.

"We had to ask him all kinds of questions to get details," said Lemieux's mother. "Mario's like that. He's always taken care of his family, and when things aren't going well, he wants to protect us."[2]

Lemieux's Pittsburgh Penguin teammates were stunned when they heard the news. They were not strangers to serious illnesses. The baby daughter of goaltender Tom Barrasso had battled leukemia, and won. Coach Bob Johnson was not so lucky. He had died of brain cancer just a few months after leading the Penguins to their first Stanley Cup championship in 1991.

Although doctors told Lemieux they had caught the disease at an early stage and there was a 95 percent chance of his surviving, he was troubled. His family had a tragic history of cancer. Two uncles and a cousin had died of cancer, one of them from Hodgkin's disease. Lemieux, however, tried to remain positive.

But Lemieux had never faced an opponent like this. The enemy could not be seen. Lemieux also had other problems. He had developed a lung infection that was not related to his cancer. He would need two weeks of recuperation time for that before he could begin the treatments for his disease.

Lemieux was experiencing the usual side effects of the radiation treatments—fatigue, nausea, and loss of appetite. Still, he was anxious to get back on the ice. He resumed skating only one week after starting the therapy, and was practicing as much as four times a week.

When Lemieux was forced out of the game, he had been having the best year of his NHL career. He was chasing Wayne Gretzky's season record of 215 points. Now he was just worried about catching up with Buffalo's Pat LaFontaine, who had taken over the lead in the scoring race.

Less than a month after he began radiation treatments, Lemieux asked to come back. It was too early, the Penguins said. General manager Craig Patrick: "We almost have to take the position of protecting him from himself."[3]

When Lemieux finally returned, there was no protecting LaFontaine from Lemieux's determination. LaFontaine was hot, no doubt about it. One Saturday late in the season, he had three assists to add three more points to his mounting total. He actually lost two points in the scoring race, however. Mario Lemieux picked up five points against Philadelphia. It was the second straight four-goal

Lemieux shares a congratulatory bear hug with teammate Jaromir Jagr following a Penguins' goal.

game for Lemieux. "Patty has to be getting a little nervous," Mario's Pittsburgh teammate Kevin Stevens said of LaFontaine.[4]

Mario Lemieux's playing reflected that of his team. With their big man leading the way, the Penguins ripped off an NHL-record seventeen-game winning streak at the end of the season. They finished with the best record in the league. By then Lemieux had won the scoring championship. He had come back from his illness trailing LaFontaine by twelve points. He finished twelve points ahead, even though he had played twenty-four fewer games.

However, remarkable comebacks were nothing new for Lemieux. The year before, he had suffered a broken hand in a playoff series against the Rangers, yet came back to lead the Penguins to their second straight Stanley Cup in the spring of 1992.

Now the Penguins were favored to win another under Scotty Bowman. He had taken over as coach when Johnson got sick. However, the Penguins were upset by the New York Islanders—a team that had finished 32 points behind Pittsburgh in the Patrick Division standings.

It was not the way Lemieux expected to finish the season. What happened next was also unexpected. Lemieux was back in the hospital for yet another operation. Once again, he needed back surgery. The only highlights of the summer were his MVP award for the 1992–93 season and his marriage to Nathalie Asselin, his longtime girlfriend, who had recently given birth to a baby girl.

With continuing back problems, a frustrated Lemieux missed 62 out of 84 games in 1993–94. The Penguins again missed the Stanley Cup. Then Mario made an announcement. He was taking a year off.

FACT

During the 1996–97 season, Mario Lemieux became only the seventh player in NHL history to score as many as 600 goals. Lemieux accomplished it in his 719th game, only one more than it took all-time scoring leader Wayne Gretzky to do it. Lemieux also became the fifth player with over 600 goals and 800 assists. This is how the all-time scorers stood prior to the 1997–98 season:

Members of the NHL's "600 Club"	Goals	Members of the "600/800 Club"	Goals/Assists
1. Wayne Gretzky	862	1. Wayne Gretzky	862/1,843
2. Gordie Howe	801	2. Gordie Howe	801/1,049
3. Marcel Dionne	731	3. Marcel Dionne	731/1,040
4. Phil Esposito	717	4. Phil Esposito	717/873
5. Mike Gartner	696	5. Mario Lemieux	613/881
6. Bobby Hull	610		
7. Mario Lemieux	613		

Since 1990, two back operations, a rare bone infection in his back, and Hodgkin's disease had worn down Lemieux to the point of physical and mental exhaustion. He needed to recuperate to reassess his hockey future.

Lemieux said he would only come back if he was healthy enough to play a major portion of the season. He did not want to have another year like 1993–94, when he only played about one quarter of the games.

While his teammates played the long, torturous NHL season in 1994–95, Mario Lemieux had his own torturous schedule of strengthening exercises. Determination was evident on his face as he sweated out the daily routine. He was resolved to come back, to be healthy enough to play a full NHL season again.

Finally, all that hard, off-the-ice labor paid off. Lemieux was coming back for the 1995–96 season. All eyes were on Mario Lemieux as he returned to the ice. The question persisted: How would he respond after staying away from the game for a year?

The Boston Bruins found out in a midseason game. They were leading the Penguins 6–4 with a minute left in regulation when Pittsburgh tied it on late goals by Tomas Sandstrom and Jaromir Jagr.

The Penguins had forced overtime. However, they were soon in trouble. They had to skate a man short because of a penalty to defenseman Dmitri Mironov. Lemieux was sent out on the ice as one of the Penguins' penalty killers. Lemieux had stolen the puck away from many an opposing player in such a situation to score a short-handed goal. Fifty seconds into the penalty, Lemieux stole the puck from Boston defenseman Jon Rohloff at the blue line. Soon he was skating toward the Bruins' net, barreling in on goaltender Bill Ranford.

Lemieux shot. Ranford dove. It was too late, though. The puck was past him. The Penguins had pulled out a wild 7–6 victory on Lemieux's second goal of the game and fifth game-winner of the season. If Lemieux was rusty from a year's layoff, or had lost a step, it did not show.

The season had not been totally satisfying for Lemieux, however. Despite winning another scoring championship, he felt as if he had not played his best. He took a long time to consider whether he would return for the 1996–97 season. Lemieux would turn thirty-one on the season's opening weekend. "At this stage in my career, the (Stanley) Cup is the biggest motivation." Ending the suspense, Lemieux announced he would return for one last shot at the Cup.[5]

Mario Lemieux returned for one more season in 1996, in the hopes of earning the Stanley Cup one last time.

Lemieux fell short of his goal when the Penguins were knocked out of the 1997 playoffs in the first round by the Philadelphia Flyers. By then, he had made his decision public—he would retire for good at the end of the season. Health problems continued to plague him, and he wanted to spend more time with his family. Lemieux was leaving the game he loved in the prime of his career. However, as he said, "I haven't been able to play at a high level, and that is very tough for me to take."[6] Still, Lemieux managed to win yet another scoring championship. It was his sixth in twelve seasons in the NHL. He also played in another All-Star Game. Along the way, he became only the seventh player in NHL history to score 600 goals.

Although Philadelphia beat Pittsburgh 6–3 to clinch the first-round playoff series, Flyers captain Eric Lindros felt a loss as he talked in the dressing room. Speaking of Lemieux, he said: "When one of the greatest, most skilled players leaves hockey, the game loses quality that cannot be replaced. There are few players I just love to watch play the game on television or live when I have the chance. Mario was one of them, just great fun because of what he could do. He had a special shine all his own, a charisma that made him very special. He's just one of those guys people want to see."[7]

Mario Lemieux already has his place in history. Usually, there is a three-year wait before a player can be considered for the Hockey Hall of Fame. In a surprise move, Lemieux was voted in shortly after his retirement because of his outstanding skill. His two Stanley Cups and scoring records are only part of the story. Mario Lemieux's most impressive achievements have been recorded in courageous comebacks. Time after time, he has battled what seemed to be impossible odds, and has come out a winner in every sense of the word.

Chapter Notes

Chapter 1. Back From the Brink

1. Alan Robinson, "Mario Returns," The Associated Press electronic library, news report, March 3, 1993.

Chapter 2. A Mighty Mite

1. Goose Goslin, "Renaissance Rookies," *Pittsburgh Magazine*, September 1985, p. 75.

2. Herb Zurkowsky, "Mario Lemieux: Hockey's Next Superstar?" *Montreal Gazette*, November 12, 1983, p. G-1.

3. Austin Murphy, "Make Room For Mario," *Sports Illustrated*, February 6, 1989, p. 35.

4. Ibid.

5. Alan Abraham, "Mario Lemieux: From Early Days to Man of the Year," Pittsburgh Penguin program, February 1987.

6. Larry Wigge, "A Domesticated Lemieux Picks Up Penguins," *The Sporting News*, January 27, 1986, p. 32.

7. Ibid.

Chapter 3. Chasing the Record

1. Lawrence Martin, *Mario* (Toronto: Lester Publishing, 1993), p. 61.

2. Author interview with Pierre Creamer, fall 1996.

3. Author interview with Chantal Machabee, fall 1996.

4. Ibid.

5. Author interview with Herb Zurkowsky, fall 1996.

Chapter 4. The Next Gretzky

1. E. M. Swift, "Pittsburgh Lands a Rare Bird," *Sports Illustrated*, October 15, 1984, p. 55.

2. Bob Phillips, "Mario Lemieux: Pittsburgh's Premier Penguin," *Scholastic Update*, February 9, 1987, p. 20.

3. Bob Kravitz, "The Talk of the Town," *Sports Illustrated*, March 3, 1986, p. 36.

4. Phillips, p. 20.

5. Barry Wilner, "NHL All-Stars," The Associated Press electronic library, news report, February 13, 1985.

6. Author interview with Mario Lemieux, winter 1987.

7. Kravitz, p. 40.

8. Author interview with Tom McMillan, fall 1996.

Chapter 5. World Champion

1. The Associated Press electronic library, news report on the Canada Cup, September 3, 1987.

2. The Associated Press electronic library, second news report on the Canada Cup, September 14, 1987.

3. Ibid.

4. Ibid.

5. The Associated Press electronic library, third news report on the Canada Cup, September 16, 1987.

6. Ibid.

Chapter 6. A Star Among Stars

1. Dave Molinari, "In Defense Of Mario," *Sport*, March 1988, p. 66.

2. Ken Rappoport, The Associated Press electronic library, news report on Mario Lemieux, February 10, 1988.

3. Jon Scher, "Netminder's Nightmare," *Sports Illustrated*, November 16, 1992, p. 48.

4. *The Sporting News*, "Mother Nature Snips Lemieux String at 46," February 26, 1990, p. 20.

5. Ken Rappoport, The Associated Press electronic library, news report on Mario Lemieux, February 10, 1988.

6. Alan Robinson, The Associated Press electronic library, news report on Mario Lemieux, February 15, 1990.

7. Ken Rappoport, The Associated Press electronic library, news report on Mario Lemieux, February 10, 1988.

Chapter 7. Bound for Glory

1. Larry Wigge, "Title Role," *The Sporting News*, June 8, 1992, p. 42.

2. Ibid.

3. Tom McMillan, "About Time to Play It Again, Mario," *The Sporting News*, January 21, 1991, p. 15.

4. Ibid.

5. Ken Rappoport, The Associated Press electronic library, news report on Mario Lemieux, January 27, 1991.

6. Alan Robinson, The Associated Press electronic library, news report on Mario Lemieux, May 14, 1991.

7. Larry Wigge, "Now, We're Seeing the Complete Lemieux," *The Sporting News*, May 20, 1991, p. 35.

8. Jay Greenberg, "On Top at Last," *Sports Illustrated*, June 3, 1991, p. 37.

Chapter 8. Beating the Odds

1. Alan Robinson, The Associated Press electronic library, news report on Lemieux's Hodgkin's disease, January 15, 1993.

2. Alan Robinson, The Associated Press electronic library, second news report on Lemieux's Hodgkin's disease, January 16, 1993.

3. Alan Robinson, The Associated Press electronic library, third news report on Lemieux's Hodgkin's disease, February 23, 1993.

4. The Associated Press electronic library, news report on Mario Lemieux, March 22, 1993.

5. Alan Robinson, The Associated Press electronic library, news report on Mario Lemieux, September 10, 1996.

6. John Bonfatti, The Associated Press electronic library, news report on Mario Lemieux, April 26, 1997.

7. Rich Chere, "Lemieux's Retirement Sincere . . . But Will It Last?" *The Star Ledger*, April 27, 1997, sec. 5, p. 7.

Career Statistics

Season	Team	League	GP	G	A	PTS	PIM
1984–85	Pittsburgh	NHL	73	43	57	100	54
1985–86	Pittsburgh	NHL	79	48	93	141	43
1986–87	Pittsburgh	NHL	63	54	53	107	57
1987–88	Pittsburgh	NHL	77	70	98	168	92
1988–89	Pittsburgh	NHL	76	85	114	199	100
1989–90	Pittsburgh	NHL	59	45	78	123	78
1990–91	Pittsburgh	NHL	26	19	26	45	30
1991–92	Pittsburgh	NHL	64	44	87	131	94
1992–93	Pittsburgh	NHL	60	69	91	160	38
1993–94	Pittsburgh	NHL	22	17	20	37	32
1994–95	Pittsburgh	NHL	DID NOT PLAY				
1995–96	Pittsburgh	NHL	70	69	92	161	54
1996–97	Pittsburgh	NHL	76	50	72	122	65
TOTALS			745	613	881	1,494	737

GP—Games played
G—Goals
A—Assists
PTS—Points
PIM—Penalty minutes

Where to Write
Mario Lemieux

Index

DATE DUE

JUL 2 1 1998	DEC 0 6 2004	
	MAR 2 1 2005	
SEP 0 1 1998		
DEC 2 8 1998		
FEB 1 6 1999		
APR 1 3 1999		
2 7 JAN 2000		
DEC 1 8 2000		
MAR 0 9 2001		
APR 1 8 2001		
MAY 2 2 2001		
MAR 0 2 2002		
3-25-02		
AUG 1 2 2002		
MAY 1 2 2003		
NOV 2 4 2003		

GAYLORD · PRINTED IN U.S.A.